For more information: **www.Amarantine.Life**

ISBN: (Print)   978-1-939556-37-0
ISBN: (eBook) 978-1-939556-38-7

ISSN: 2515-7434 (Online)
ISSN: 2515-7426 (Print)

I0170407

First published: May, 2018 UK

Images used throughout this book are sourced from Pixabay, Dreamstime, 123RF, PresenterMedia, Shutterstock, or Alphaspirit | Dreamstime.com.

Limit of Liability / Disclaimer of Warranty: While the authors have used their best efforts in preparing this book, they make no representations or warranties with respect to the accuracy or completeness of the contents and specifically disclaim any implied warranties. The authors shall not be liable for any loss of profit or any other commercial or

EXPECTATIONS

The Expectation Gap

How can expectations help or hinder you?

Managing Editor:
Denny Portier-Terpstra

Contributors:
Jenny Schmal
Barbara J. Cormack
Bettina Pickering
Curly Martin
Loren Schmal
Alyson Daley
Dr. Charuni Senanayake

Contents

Denny's Deliberations

by

Denny Portier-Terpstra

I feel that "expectations" are a rather tricky emotion, as it can set us up for both failure and success. And there seems to be a delicate balance in there, which can be pretty hard to find at times.

When you have low expectations of yourself and your capabilities, you can be sure that you won't have success. When you don't expect that you'll ever lose the weight, you are more likely to eat that extra cookie, because there's little point in leaving it out of your diet. When you expect that you'll never be promoted to the next level at work, you are less likely to invest in acquiring the required skills and knowledge for the role and to apply for the opportunity when it presents itself. And so on… With low expectations, you are likely to achieve low results, as it will become a self-fulfilling prophecy.

And equally so, higher expectations can help you achieve better results. When you truly believe that you can run that marathon, you will train hard and put your best foot forward to achieving it, which increases your chances of indeed reaching that finish line. When you expect a good result, you probably won't settle for anything less, and your focus and determination will do the rest. As such, high expectations can become a self-fulfilling prophecy too.

However, where things may get awkward, is when we set our expectations wrong. Expecting too much will likely lead to failure and disappointment instead of achievement, and expecting too little may mean that you'll sell yourself short (although it can lead to a welcome surprise occasionally as well).

In this issue of Amarantine, we will explore what expectations are and how they can help or hinder us in achieving the desired results.

Happy reading!

Warmest regards,
Denny

Denny Portier-Terpstra
Managing Editor Amarantine

"High achievement always takes place in the framework of high expectation."

Charles Kettering

Why Hope is a Hopeless Strategy!

by
Jenny Schmal

In the 1986 film "Clockwise", the principal character is *en-route* to deliver the most important speech of his life, but misses his train. The subsequent sequence of events make for great comedic effect, as he frantically attempts to get to the venue at the appointed hour, and the rising sense of frustration and panic become almost unbearable as the seconds tick away. As he sees the last opportunities slip from his grasp, he muses; "It's not the despair; I can take the despair. It's the hope I can't stand."

As in all good comedy, the humor arises from our recognition of the underlying truth. For what is 'hope', other than a futile longing for circumstances we feel powerless to change? Hope is one of those words that convey the opposite meaning to that intended: 'Hope' really means 'hopelessness'.

If our expectations are based on hope, we infer that we are at the mercy of circumstances beyond our control. We have removed ourselves from the ability to influence the outcome.

Are you living in hope?

Notice how often you prefix a wish or an intention with the words "I hope....", and notice how it casts a subtle shadow of doubt over the predicted event. Take a few moments to reflect on just how often you use the words 'I hope'.

"I hope to see you soon."

"I hope I remember to buy milk."

"I hope to finish this report by Tuesday."

"Will you be at the meeting on Friday?" "I hope so."

Do you see how the words 'I hope' are neither necessary nor useful in the above statements?" You could just as easily say:

"See you soon."

"I must remember to buy milk."

"I intend to finish this report by Tuesday."

"Will you be at the meeting?" "Yes."

How many times in a day do you limit your achievements by adding the shackles of *hope*? Have you let go of creating your life by design and just settled for the 'safety' of 'he who does not expect will never be disappointed?'

Hope is a low vibrational state of fear – the fear of not getting what you want.

Where does that fear come from? The fear of setting firm intentions stems from previous experiences where you set intentions, and limit the outcome to arriving in one particular way, at one particular time.

If it didn't happen the way you wanted it to, you assumed that you had failed - at the time. Your belief that you had failed **created** your experience of disappointment.

However, how many times, in hindsight, did you discover that **not** getting that outcome at that time turned out to be the best thing that could have happened? Or, that you did get the outcome, but in a better way or at a better time?

Limiting the outcome to one set of circumstances does not allow for factors such as:
- it's not the right time yet
- something else has to happen first
- something bigger and better is on its way!

You will never be able to eliminate bad things from happening, but, if

you sit back and wait for events to unfold, you throw yourself at the mercy of fate. The doubt that it will happen, allows the mind to dwell on and create the circumstances that *will* prevent it happening.

Can you see how powerfully your words can sabotage your results?

Abandon Hope!

The next time you declare an intention, eliminate hope from the equation. Open your mind to the possibility that the outcome may arrive the way you want or that something better will happen. Go ahead and perform the action necessary to bring about the intention.

You are now operating from the much higher vibrational state of **anticipation**.

Anticipation is the knowledge that you are diligently applying the steps to design and implement your desired intention, and that there are only two possible outcomes:

You get what you wanted

You get something better

Stop wasting your time — and your life — in fear of disappointment.

Take your power back; become a 'no-hoper'!

Jenny Schmal
© 2018 Jenny Schmal

Jenny Schmal ASC is available for private coaching, corporate events, and can be booked as a motivational speaker.

"We will always tend to fulfill our own expectation of ourselves."

Brian Tracy

The Power of Expectation

Step-by-Step Series

by

Barbara J. Cormack

"Expectation is
the mother of all frustration."
Antonio Banderas

As part of taking one step at a time to achievement and success, it's important to look back and review what you've achieved so far and recognise how far you have come in your goal to make changes in your life.

Your Journey is the topic of our conversations in this series of articles. Your Wheel of Life through your own Soul Searching helped you identify what is in your life today by creating your own life segments and where you are within those; followed by what you would like to incorporate, include, or even release from each segment. This process allowed you to start identifying what is right and what is missing from each segment of your life. By taking the three most important segments you started to become clear about your inner most dream(s) or aspiration(s). Writing down a short sentence about each dream or aspiration helps you to clarify what it is you truly want from those segments of your life. In the last issue I asked 'If you can't say 'no' to the things or circumstances or situations or people you don't want in your life, who will?'

The reason for following through this process and asking you that particular question gives you the opportunity to really look at and identify WHY you want to make these changes.

The why is the key to success.

"Life
is largely a matter of expectation."
Horace

The Power of Expectation determines what you have in and do with your life. If you expect to be a success, you will be. Equally if you expect to fail, you will do. Where do these expectations come from? With many different people involved in your busy life, one of the questions you have to ask is 'whose expectation'?

At school, the expectation was that you were the same as the child next to you in class. You had the same upbringing. Your parents had the same level of income to be able to buy what you needed. You had the same interests. You had the same understanding of the world. Your parents had the same expectation of you that their parents had of them, or their friends have of their children – you will get 'A' results in all exams; you are incredibly successful at all sports; and you win all the competitions.

Later in life other people have expectations of you! Your 'significant other' has their own expectations of you. Your children have their expectations of you. Your friends have their expectations of you. Your boss has their expectation of you. Your colleagues have their expectations of you. And yes the list goes on … expectations are not only your own expectations of yourself, but mixed in are everyone else's expectations of you too.

I am at an interesting point in my life, where right now we are designing our own home. We have bought a plot of land with planning permission and are trying to work out what interior we want in our house. In doing this exercise we both have expectations. I expect to have a study that provides me with exactly what I want in terms of space and storage. My partner expects to have a garage, workshop, and study that provides him with exactly what he wants in terms of space and storage. Easy – two sets of expectations that can come together. BUT what about the rest of the house? It was only as we were pulling together outline drawings that we realised how different our own thoughts and expectations were for this house. I want something that is light and airy. My partner wants something that is light and airy, but easy to build in terms of placing windows. For me, I was letting my imagination run wild. As an engineer, he was thinking about the engineering aspect first and then the design. Although we haven't yet got to our final plan, we both believe that we can have something that fulfils both our expectations. It's the Power of Expectation that gives us this confidence.

Simply put, the Power of Expectation (or thinking about this in terms of Universal Laws, the Law of Expectation) is belief, energy, and emotion. What you 'expect' for your life, if you expect it with belief, positive energy, and positive emotions; you will get it.

The challenge of the power of expectation comes from your own self-limiting beliefs, self-doubts, and often if the expectation is not yours but someone else's that they have 'given' to you.

Looking back at the sentence you wrote down for your dream(s) or aspiration(s), it is important to identify whose dream or aspiration it is. If it is not yours, but someone else's dream or aspiration for you, be clear! This will be true of business, and in some cases career goals. In the main, these goals are set by the Business Owners or Board of Directors; and are passed down through the chain of leadership to each person in the team. These type of goals are a whole different conversation, but are important to your overall expectations of you.

Sometimes a dream or aspiration is a shared one. As in my case, building our own dream house is a shared aspiration.

Sometimes a dream or aspiration is one which in your inner most heart you know will upset someone else, and maybe even change your relationship with one or more people.

Sometimes a dream or aspiration is something you have coveted all your life, but never felt that you could achieve it, share it, have it, be it, or do it.

Before we move on and talk more about the Power of Expectations, go back to the dream(s) or aspiration(s) that you wrote down; and ask yourself whose is it?

- Yours only

- Yours in partnership with someone else

- Someone else's, and if so, whose.

**"Whatever the mind
can conceive and believe,
it can achieve,"
Napoleon Hill**

Now that you know whose dream or aspiration you have written down, ask yourself 'why have I selected this dream or aspiration?' The 'why' question is the most important question you can ask yourself. It will help you reveal reasons, conflicts, previous results that haven't been successful; and is the question that exposes the purpose. It's often referred to as the 'justification' question. If you don't have an answer to the 'why' question, then maybe this is not the right dream or aspiration? Maybe the first question you should be asking is 'why have I written down this dream or aspiration'? Maybe now is the time to reflect on that particular question and if necessary change your dream or aspiration to the right one. If the answer is 'because I have to do it for work', how do you change your dream or aspiration sentence to one that gives you the 'why' answer of something more motivating to you!

**"The mind is everything.
What you think,
you become."
Buddha**

Now that you know and have agreed with the 'why', re-write the sentence to include the important elements of the 'why'. Remember that the Power of Expectation basically states that whatever you presume with positive belief, positive energy, and positive emotion; you will achieve. So, take this time to write out your sentence in a way that when

16

you look at it, speak it out loud, or think it in your mind; it energises you.

Write your sentence as an affirmation. Affirmations are simply positive statements written down and regularly stated that are simple, positive statements declaring that your dream or aspiration has happened.

- From your perspective. Start the sentence with 'I'.
- In the present. So write it sentence as though the dream or affirmation is happening right now in your life. i.e. 'I have …' and not 'I will have …'.
- Positively. Write it as though you have it now, and not from the perspective of what you don't want in your goal or aspiration.
- With belief. You know in your inner most heart that your dream or aspiration is yours!
- With positive energy. You know in your inner most heart that you deserve your dream or aspiration.
- With a light hearted, positive emotion. You know that in your inner most heart that this one thing will allow you to lead the life you believe you are entitled to lead.

Although this may sound really simple, to support your beliefs and habits, you need to turn your affirmation(s) into a mantra. By repeating your mantra or mantras first thing in the morning, at every break, refreshment or meal, and in the evening, and as you go to bed; you will experience a change of negative habits of thinking 'this can't happen' to positive habits to 'another step and this has happened'. Mantras repeated regularly throughout the day has a profound effect on both your conscious and sub-conscious mind.

Your beliefs are your foundation of your unconscious thoughts, your feelings, and your self-image. If your thoughts are generally negative thoughts, then your feelings are generally that of 'I can't …' and your self-image is often a negative self-image. Your beliefs are the reason you make the decisions you make, you take the actions you take, you respond in the manner you do.

So how do you move from 'I can't …' to 'I have …'?

Your affirmations said (out loud or in your mind) with absolute positive belief, positive energy, and positive emotion; are one step. The research published in 2015, in the Personality and Social Psychology Bulletin, demonstrates how affirmations can be successful. Other research though demonstrates that when an affirmation is said or thought without the belief; it can have a negative effect.

If you have any questions or doubts about your affirmations, work on the reason 'why'. Sometimes the questions or doubts come from knowing that someone may get hurt if you make this change. Sometimes the questions or doubts come from long term negative thinking or beliefs. Sometimes the questions or doubts come from not believing that you are entitled to achieve your own dreams or aspirations. Whatever the reason, until you believe in your own future, written down in your affirmations, you will always put a block in your own way.

Writing about achieving your own dreams always brings back my own changes. It is sometimes easier to make a decision not to make a change in your life because by making the change you may hurt someone that you don't want to hurt. In some of the decisions I took in my life, I did hurt others and it was not an easy decision. Years later when

I look back, their hurt was short lived as the person or people impacted by my decision began to understand the reason for my decision, my actions, and my changes; and the positive effect it had on their life, as well as my own. At the time, it was not easy to make that decision; nor was it easy to communicate it. As I look back today, I know that if I had not made that decision, not communicated my choice; I would be both stuck in a relationship and also in a place in my life, which was not a happy place.

If you really don't want to make these changes, then take the stress away from your life; and don't make the changes. If you really do want to make these changes; moving from 'I can't …' to 'I have …' is a step-by-step process that you will follow. It is something that will happen if you select to let it.

Take the one dream or aspiration that you feel is your top most priority: the one and only one that will make the biggest change in your life. Look at the affirmation statement you have written down and ask yourself – 'am I entitled to have this?' If your INSTANT answer is not 'YES' with a feeling of overwhelming happiness, ask yourself 'why not?'

One of the secrets to success is truly knowing what is stopping you; what is blocking you; what is the absolute reason you have not made this change before.

For this specific dream or aspiration, make a list of all the things that you do NOT want. Now make a list of all the things that you do want.

Using this list, close your eyes and visualise yourself living your dream or aspiration. In your visualisation, see what you are wearing, see where you are, see what you are doing, listen to what you are saying, see who is with you, see what they are wearing, see what they are doing, and listen to what they are saying. Visualise yourself living the life of your dream or aspiration.

With this picture in your mind, capture all the details from your visualisation. Once you have all the information written down, go back to your affirmation and re-write it – with a positive belief that you can live the life you select to live.

Now, when you say your affirmation during the day; bring your visualisation back to your mind. As you are saying your affirmation, see yourself living your dream or aspiration.

This positive visualisation with a positive statement will have a huge effect on your conscious mind, sub-conscious mind, and your body. You will start to knock down those limiting beliefs and replace them with positive beliefs. You will know away that unsure and doubting energy and replace it with a positive energy. When you visualise your future, your emotions will begin to change from a position of where you are today to the feeling of happiness, lightness, and positive emotions.

The power of positive thought will impress upon your mind the actions that you need to take, which in turn will impress upon your body what you physically need to do, to take the actions.

As you take each action and move one step at a time towards your dream or aspiration, your belief in your dream or aspiration will increase and your expectations will change from 'I can't have this dream or aspiration', to 'I can and will have this dream or aspiration.' Before you know it, you will be living your dream or aspiration.

It may sound easy, but only you can remove the ceiling in your mind which is stopping you from living your aspired life, by taking one step at a time to establish positive beliefs, positive energies, and positive emotions. Only you can change the power of expectation from 'I can't ...' to 'I have ...'.

Simply follow this process for a minimum of 30 consecutive days:

1. Create your affirmation with positive belief, positive energy, and positive emotion.
2. Create your visualisation of you living your dream or aspiration.
3. Repeat your affirmation, with your visualisation in your mind, with positive belief, positive energy, and positive emotion; for at least five minutes three times a day.

Barbara J. Cormack
© 2018 Barbara J. Cormack

Barbara J. Cormack AFC, AFM, MNMC is an award winning coach, an author, mentor, trainer, and a sought after international speaker.

*"Carry out a random act of kindness,
with no expectation of reward,
safe in the knowledge that one day
someone might do the same for you."*

Princess Diana

Perspective

Self-care

On our early morning walk, I realised that the position of the moon was a great way to understand the perspective on EXPECTATIONS!

In the early morning dawn, as we walked out the front door, the moon was clearly visible behind the house. As we walked down the track from our gate; away from the house which was behind us, the moon was visible to my right. We walked up the track towards our turn-around point and the moon was visible at all times. I turned around to get bearing on where the house was and it appeared as though the moon was moving across the sky giving us clear visibility of it all the time, but now no-where near our house. Having reached our turn-around point (at the top of the hill), on turning around the position of the moon became clear again. We stopped to get our bearings. The moon was directly in front of us. The house was down in the valley to our right. Had the moon moved?

It made me realise that for each one of us, our expectations move daily!

In this issue of Amarantine you will read a number of articles that will help you understand your own expectations. Whether these are your own expectations or expectations from someone/somewhere else, they are based on not only your self-belief, but also on your goals.

What happens when someone challenges you about one of your goals? Often the goal will change. It may grow larger if the challenge has been 'is that all you think you can have?' or it may reduce if the challenge has been 'what, that much?'. If, based on the challenge, you have looked at your goal and changed it; your expectations change.

At a conference many years ago, one of the presenters was talking about achieving his goal; without actually realising it. In a magazine he had seen an article about a house. He and his wife agreed that was the house they would love to live in – their dream home. He cut out all the articles and pasted them on a vision board. He put the vision on the wall in his study and looked at it every day.

A couple of years later they needed to move house. Having sold their house, they started to pack up. He took his vision board off the wall, rolled it up and put it in the cardboard tube so that it could move with them to the new house. A lot of their cardboard boxes went into storage – the loft, the garage, etc. They were never opened. A second move. A third move. By this time, they had 'forgotten' about their dream home. After their first move, their expectations changed to finding a home that suited their requirements. A further move and they both decided that every single box would need to be opened and decisions made. All these boxes kept moving with them and by now, many years later, they couldn't remember what was in some of them. Over a period of time they worked through each box. He came to the cardboard tube, opened it up and pulled out his vision board. WOW! He rushed through to his wife and showed her the vision board. YES, they were now living in their dream home.

So, do your expectations change?

The moon is in one place in the sky. It does not move left and right. It does not change position. It is my perspective of the position of the moon that changes; and not my expectation.

This is not an easy question, as expectations are based on goals and self-belief. If you really, truly believe that you can have your goal; then your expectations will not change. The path you take to achieve that goal may not be a straight and narrow path; it maybe twisty and windy with many deviations and stops. If you truly believe you will achieve your goal and your expectations are set; you will!

Unconscious Expectations:
the eternal
Hamster Wheel of Feeling
"Not Good Enough"

by
Bettina Pickering

Have you ever been plagued by a sense of never being good enough?

Never being the person you know you should be?

Feeling pressure that never seems to be letting up?

Run off your feet yet never arriving anywhere?

If that is you, you might be carrying expectations of yourself that are in the main unconscious. Some people call this "perfectionist syndrome", others call it "imposter syndrome", yet other call it "high achiever syndrome". And there are many other names.

I call it: the disease of unconscious expectations.

Why?

If you have total clarity of what you expect from yourself on any given day you make empowered decisions and do the following:
- ☐ Delegate
- ☐ Work smarter
- ☐ Reschedule
- ☐ Build a roadmap or plan
- ☐ Outsource
- ☐ Let it go

If you don't know or only have a vague idea what you expect from yourself, you can never achieve those expectations. You will always fall short. You will always underperform.

Let's explore those unconscious expectations we have of ourselves. Those that just sit below the surface, just beyond our conscious awareness. Those that run like a never-ending hamster wheel at the backs of our minds. Those expectations, if we were asked to explain, we could not quite put words to.

Let's backtrack a bit.

When you do great, when you meet your goals for the day, or achieve more than you expected, what is that like?

Clients report that feel they are in the flow, on top of the world, happy, enjoying life, relaxed, at ease…..and I am sure you have your own words for this state.

Internally, our brain excretes oxytocin, the feel good hormone. Oxytocin makes us expand, at ease and feel good about ourselves. It also helps us learn new things with ease and find creative solutions when things don't go our way. Feeling good about ourselves produces more of the same feelings, and thus helps us to be more productive.

Conversely, when we direct anger, disappointment or frustration at ourselves, or when we feel stressed or under pressure through our own expectations, our flight, flight or freeze response is triggered in our brain through the Amygdala. Not only does this flood our body with stress hormones, causing us to contract, potentially breathe more shallowly and reduces various organs from functioning properly. What also happens is that the centres of the brain where we make good decisions, find creative solutions and learn new things, get switched off. Our concentration and focus suffer. This means we become a lot less productive.

The problem is that once we are on the Hamster Wheel of unmet expectations, we become less and less productive, and thus keep beating ourselves up, creating more and more stress hormone and less feel good hormones.

Getting off the external Hamster Wheel

How do we stop said Hamster Wheel that keeps us stuck in feeling "Not Good Enough"?

The answer is, we don't.

We don't even want to try and stop it. That takes far too much effort and leads to failure. It is a fundamental human process that can be really useful if we know how to harness its power for the right things.

Harnessing your Hamster Wheel

It will take a little work and effort on our part at least once or twice a day. The good news is that it will take less than 5 mins each time.

Now the bad news:

You have to consciously commit to those 5 minutes at the beginning and at the end of each day until it becomes an unconscious habit.

On the following pages I outline the three step process that I use myself.

Step 1: Make your expectations conscious

"Expectations are dangerous
when they are both
too high and unformed."
Lionel Shriver,
We Need to Talk About Kevin

If we don't know what we are measuring ourselves against, we will likely never succeed. You cannot get to a specific destination if you don't know what it is, or at least some of the co-ordinates of that destination.

Imagine you are in a car with a passenger who you need to drop off at their destination. You go a little way, then but the friend says: "This is not where I want to go". Try again. You go a little further, maybe take a right. Again, the friend says to you "You are not there yet". You failed. Again, you travel further, this time you try different places, just in case. You are falling short, again. Finally, after many detours and failures, your friend says: "We are here, why didn't you get me here in the first place?".

This is how we treat ourselves. We have unconscious expectations of:
- How much we should be able to get done in a day
- How well we should perform each day without fail
- What we should notice or automatically remember
- What emotions are associated with each expectation, especially when we don't meet them
- And so on....

For everything that you do or aim to do, identify, as best as you can, your expectations of yourself. Write them down.

Initially this will take a little time, and you may not identify all expectations. Don't worry, you can identify the expectations also at the point of feeling not good enough, less than or frustrated with yourself.

As a bonus, identify the expectations you have of others and/or of life in general. If we don't know consciously what we expect of others or life, we are unable to state our needs or if those expectations are unrealistic and make other arrangements.

Once you are clear of your expectations, you can bring in a good dose of realism:
- Are these expectations realistic for today?
- How much time is needed truthfully for each activity?
- What is the minimum that I could feel good about?
- What about down time? Or catch up time? Or time to deal with the unexpected?

Be ruthless and remove expectations that do not serve you, are unrealistic or that you would not have of others but for some reason you have of yourself. Your daily to do list will shrink due to this exercise, I promise.

Step 2: Take control – book end your day

Be super clear and firm as to what goes into the Hamster Wheel at the start of your day. That is your left side book end, if you imagine your day on a shelf in front of you extending from left to right.

Use the next part of your 5 minutes at the beginning of your day to identify 1 expectation of yourself for the day. Define it. Be clear about what it means to achieve this 1 expectation. Leave no room for confusion or gaps. Make it watertight.

These 5 minutes are the most crucial 5 minutes of your day, so make them count!

At the end of the day, your right-hand bookend, use 60 seconds to acknowledge your expectation and how you did against it.

What did you do that day?

What did you achieve?

If you did not achieve what you set out to do, re-examine your expectations of yourself.

Step 3: Make a DONE list

I hate to do lists. They never end. Those people who know me, know I have loads of to do lists, so I don't forget what is on my plate. However, I am one of those people who don't find satisfaction in losing things, striking things off, rubbing things out. I like adding things onto a list. Oops.

You can imagine now what my problem is: Ever growing lists that never actually shrink.

So, I came up with the DONE list.

I designed a lovely form with 5 sections that represent the core focus areas I want to work on, my mega goals. Each section has 5 lines with space for DONE's. That way I make sure that I do at least one thing to further my goals each day. You can choose how many mega goals you want to have, and what those are for you. I would advise not to choose more than 5 as it becomes too unwieldy.

DAILY DONE LIST

GET PAID BUSINESS

EXERCISE – STRENGTHEN MY BODY

HOUSE KEEPING / FINANCES

PROGRESS CURRENT CLIENT WORK

PROGRESS CURRENT PROJECTS

Right now, for example, I work with 3 mega goals as each of them is very big in its own right.

You can download the DONE list word document with my compliments - **www.bettinapickering.com/DONELIST**. You can also download my mega goals setting process via that link.

I print my DONE list off. You can draw one yourself on an A4 or A5 piece of paper. You can also explore buying a specialist to do list book and repurpose that as a DONE list if you prefer. Or you can use electronic versions.

I find it immensely satisfying to write done my completed actions! I write my DONE's down with an elegant fountain pen. That makes it feel special and turns it into a small celebration.

When you do these three steps every day you will see results. Don't even look at your main to do list. If you are like me, you might even have several. Focus on one day at a time, on your expectations and activities, and only that day.

Bettina Pickering

© 2018 Bettina Pickering

Bettina Pickering is a transformative leadership coach, entrepreneur mentor, business transformation and change consultant, author and speaker.

"*I have a very high expectation*
for everything I do.
And when I go out and compete,
I expect myself to make every play."

Colin Kaepernick

Our Expected View of Our World!

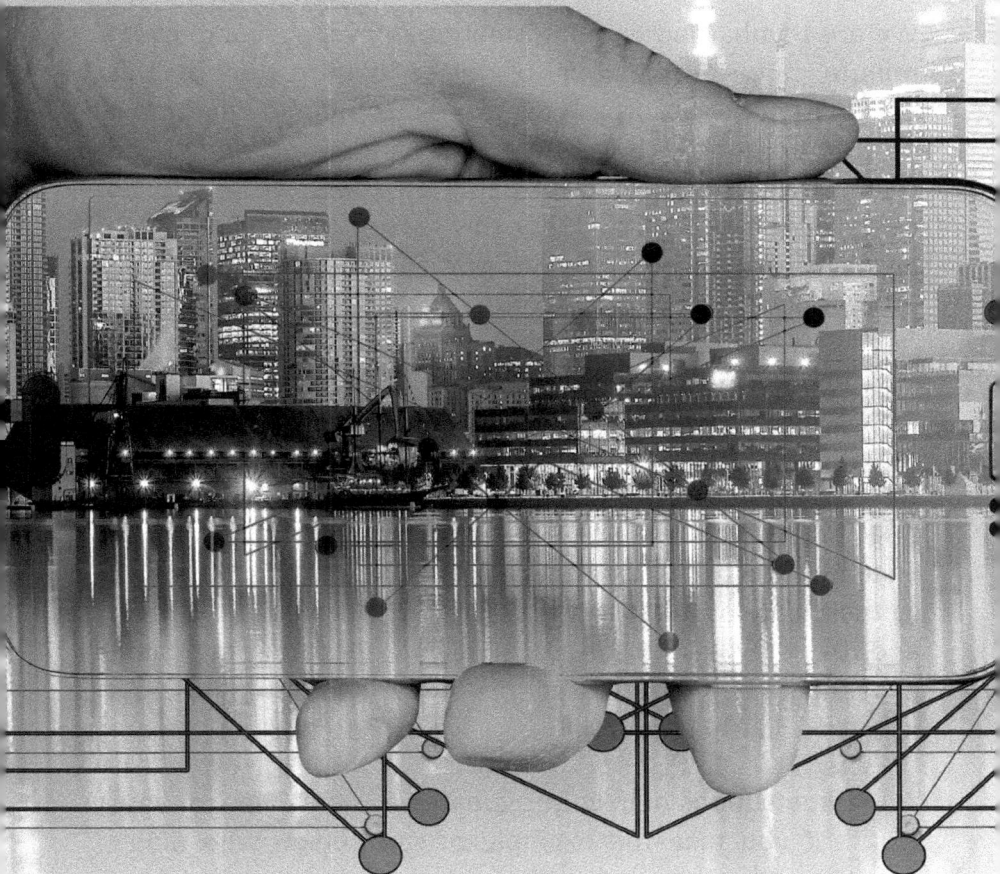

Tools, Models, Techniques

**"Our view of the world is truly shaped
by what we decide to hear".
William James**

We create our own view of our world through our five
senses – sight, hearing, touch, taste, and smell. In other
words, through our own experiences.

We are bombarded with information in every second, every
minute, and every hour of every day. A lot of this
information is absorbed by our unconscious mind and
deleted or ignored. If we were to try and acknowledge and
think about this huge level of information, we would be
completely overwhelmed. For this reason, we are not even
aware of our unconscious decision to delete or ignore the
information.

The information we select to filter, we do so with our own
beliefs and values. As an example; you might select to go
into a fast food restaurant for a quick meal. You may select
to see this meal as an unusual treat and enjoy it. Someone
else may make the same decision and feel awful, because
instead of recognising this as an unusual treat and enjoying
it, their view of the world makes them believe that it's bad
and that they will put on extra weight. By taking this same
experience, two different people create two different views
of the world: their own views.

Your expectations help you to create your own view of your
world. If you take the example of the person who didn't
enjoy their fast food meal, they have a belief that fast food
is bad for you. They did not expect to enjoy it. Even if they
enjoyed the taste, their expectation was such that they
chose to create a view of the world that said that they did
not enjoy it. What would happen if they were to actually

admit that they had enjoyed their fast food meal?

**"You can take the boy out of the country,
but you can't take the country
out of the boy ..."
It's my Life (Charlie Daniels Band)**

Recently I was talking to someone who had just had a cataract (eye) operation. With surprise, this person turned to me and said: 'the colour of that gas flame is not grey, but blue'. Over the years, as the eyes had deteriorated, this person had come to accept that the colour of the gas flame was grey, because it was in that person's view of the world. This person had not expected it to be any different, and had never asked what my view of the gas flame was. Now this person knows that we had different views.

It's very easy for you to assume that everyone has the same view of the world as you do, but they don't. Each person interprets what they see, hear, feel, touch, and taste in their own way.

A fast food meal seen as a treat and enjoyed; or guiltily. A gas flame seen as grey and blue.

**"A world view is
probably an expression of self."
Michael Leunig**

Go with someone and take your journal to a place where you can both quietly sit and watch the world go by. Open your journal and:

Focusing on the environment around you; capture where you are, what you are seeing, what you are hearing, what you are smelling, what you are tasting, what you are touching, and what you are feeling.

Now ask the person you are with to do the same — capture where they are, what they are seeing, what they are hearing, what they are smelling, what they are tasting, what they are touching, and what they are feeling.

Before you compare what you have written:

what is your expectation of what they have written?

what is their expectation of what you have written?

Now compare!

Which version of the world is right?

"You can take the boy out of Philly,
but not Philly out of the boy.
It shapes my world view."
Steve Capus

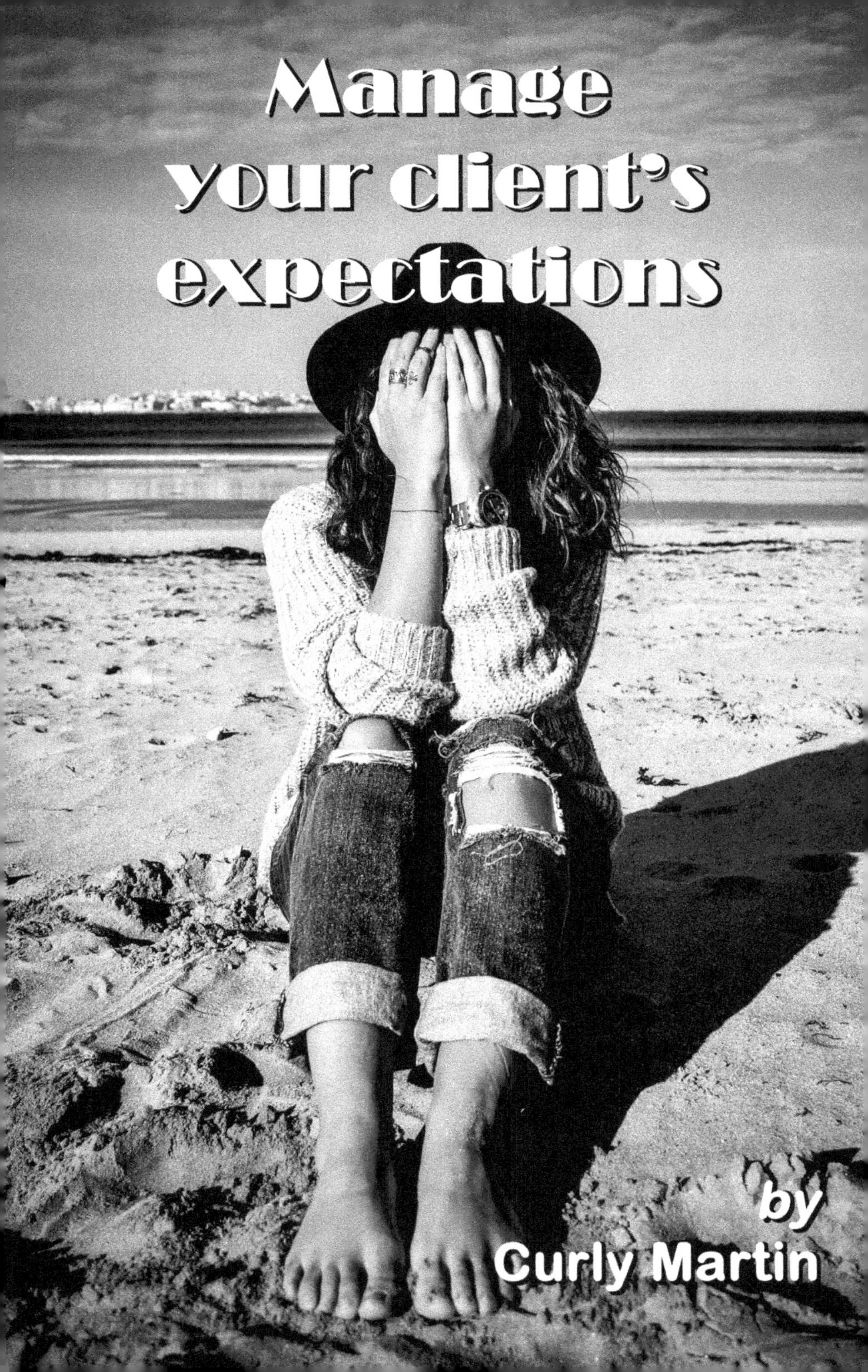
Manage
your client's
expectations
by
Curly Martin

In any type of business, it's important to manage your client's expectations. As I'm in the business of coaching coaches, I will explain this from my own perspective.

Client expectations are the main challenge brought to me by coaches when they have a client who is causing some problems. Usually the problems stem from a situation where the coach has one set of expectations for the coaching programme and the client has a differing set of expectations. This arises when the coach has forgotten to send out all the standard pieces of documentation such as; client contract, code of conduct for coach and client, business charter, terms and conditions, etc.).

The problems seem to come from the coach not fully treating coaching as a professional business and being far too relaxed about the process. This happens when a coach handles a coaching session more like a catch-up chat rather than a fully structured business service. It is my strong recommendation that all coaches consider themselves professional business service providers from the onset. All clients must be sent contractual service agreements along with other business documentation; coaches trained by me have access to many different templates for all the types of business documentation via our coaches Achievers Club.

On the diploma course I stress that all coaches must send to their clients an **_explicit_** contract which states the type of coaching programme purchased, the number and length of time of sessions, cancellation or not turning up for a session procedure, the number of emails/texts/telephone calls accepted in-between each session and all and any relevant processes or procedures discussed during the initial conversations.

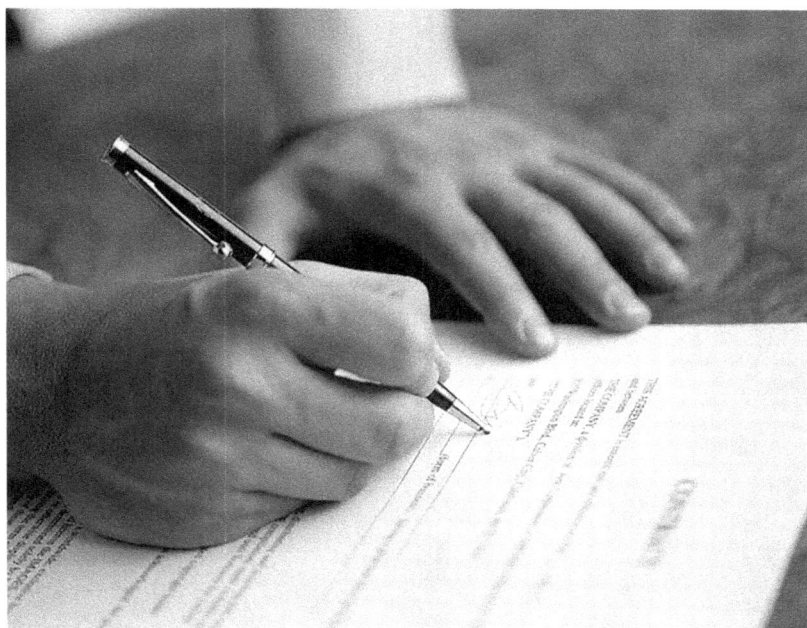

As a coach, if you do not have a clearly stated service contract you will be walking into problems with your eyes wide open. Different clients have different expectations of you, and these expectations need to be clearly expressed and always put into a written format.

For example, a coach who told the client during the initial set up conversations that if the client did not give 48-hour notice of cancellation or rescheduling of a session, the particular session would be forfeit. This means that there would be no refund and no free rescheduling of said session. This example, in practice could be construed as a verbal contract. If you have no audio recording of this conversation, nor have you followed up the conversation with written clarification of what was discussed and agreed, it will end up being your word against your client.

Nine times out of ten, your client is going to forget you ever

said anything about cancelled sessions and he or she will be very angry when you try to implement the forfeit. This is not a situation you want to find yourself in and one which can be easily avoided by producing a simple contract, having codes of conduct and terms and conditions of business.

This might sound like a lot of work and in the initial stages of setting up your coaching business this will take time. However, once you have templates created and your terms and conditions are displayed on your website the job is nearly done. The only actions you will need to take is to adjust the contract to reflect the specific client details and the processes and procedures you both agreed during the initial conversations. In my model of the world, coaching should not take place until both parties agree on the contractual way forward. Clarity equals customer satisfaction.

Curly Martin
© 2018 Curly Martin

Curly Martin, MAOC, MSFB, MSOA, AFC, AFM is a best-selling author, a sought after international speaker, and a pioneer of Life Coaching in Europe.

"Peace begins when expectation ends."
Sri Chinmoy

**"If you accept
the expectations of others,
especially negative ones,
then you never
will change the outcome."**
Michael Jordan

What is the Expectation Effect?
**"A phenomenon in which
perception and *behaviour*
change as a result of
personal expectations."**
ANON

"Winners make a habit of manufacturing their own positive expectations in advance of the event."
Brian Tracy

"I have learned that as long as I hold fast to my beliefs and values – and follow my own moral compass – then the only expectations I need to live up to are my own."
Michelle Obama

"TRADE your expectation for APPRECIATION and the world CHANGES for you."
Anthony Robbins

"Don't lower your expectations to meet your performance. Raise your level of performance to meet your expectations."

Ralph Marston

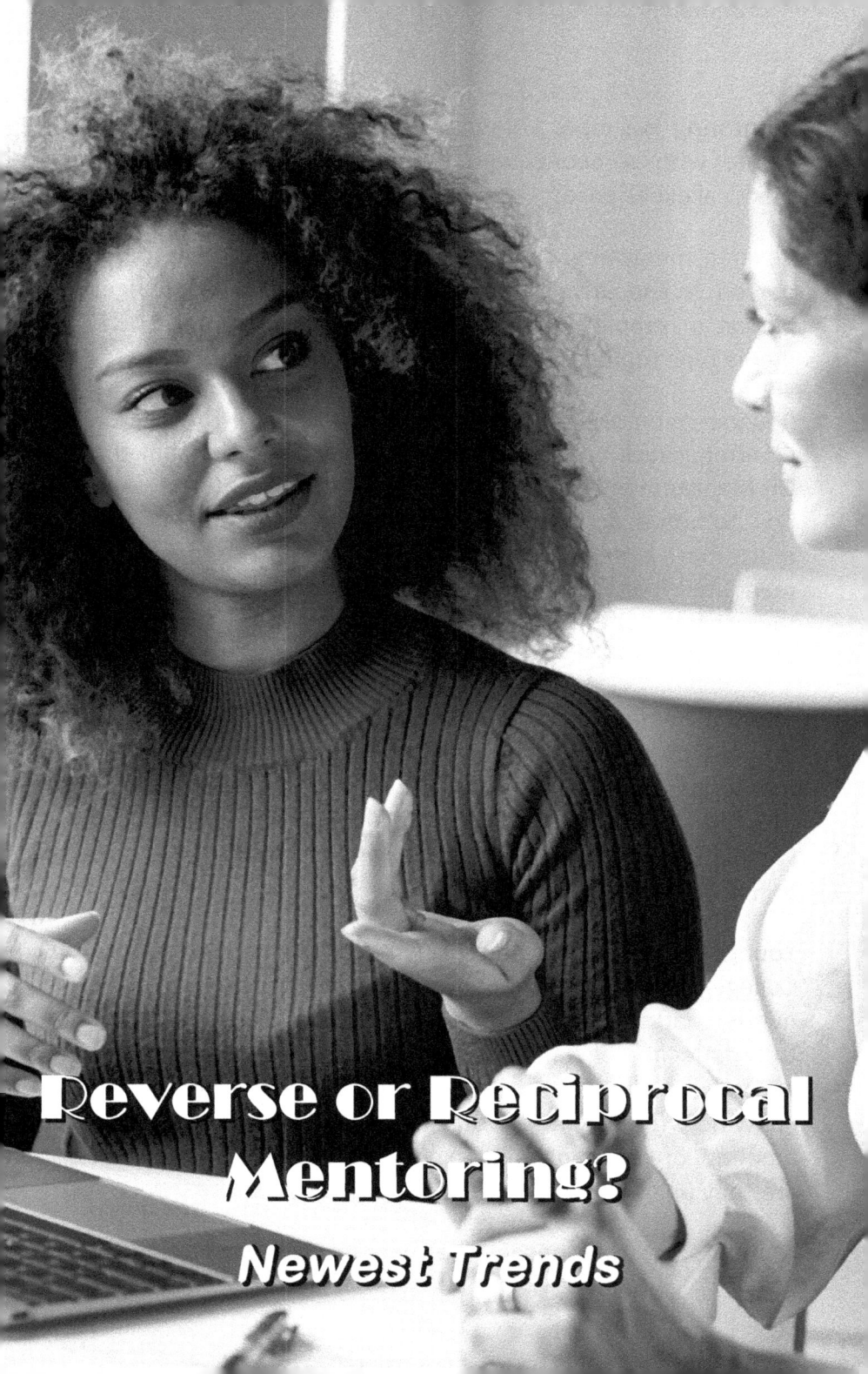

Reverse or Reciprocal Mentoring?

Newest Trends

Mentoring is simply a younger person or employee being paired with someone who is generally older with more practical experience.

Reverse mentoring on the other hand is where the older person or executive is paired and mentored by a younger person or employee, specifically on technology and social media type topics.

Reverse mentoring was first popularised by former GE Chairman, Jack Welch. In the 1990's, Jack realised that the GE Management had much to learn about the internet, and how to better do this than to learn from someone who has much more experience and knowledge about the topic. Jack mandated that GE's top executives, including himself, paired themselves with someone younger who had more experience and knowledge about the internet.

While a number of the older executives in companies feel insulted by a younger employee 'teaching' them through mentoring, Jack's example at GE went a long way to ease how the older executives were feeling; to the point where some older executives in the larger companies are now asking for younger mentors.

Younger employees, even those straight out of University or College, come into an organisation with fresh eyes, open minds, and an in-depth knowledge and experience of today's technology and social media. Those employees and executives who have been working for many years may know how the business 'works today' and have gained huge amounts of knowledge and experience in their industry; but are they up to date with today's world?

A mentoring relationship that works both ways can be

hugely beneficial to both parties, as well as to the organisation:

- Allowing each person – younger and older – in this relationship to mentor the other, closes the knowledge gap for both parties. For example, the younger person learns how a business actually works, business terminology, and industry practices; while the older person learns about the ins and outs of the internet, search engines and algorithms, social media, and mobile phone apps.

- This empowers both parties – the older person in feeling more comfortable with the changes coming into their business world; and the younger person who is learning from business leaders. The business is now grooming their future and emerging leadership team; as well as encouraging the Millennials to remain with the company. This is important, as the 2016 Deloitte Millennial Survey highlights that the millennial generation will move from company to company to grow their knowledge and experience, especially where the millennials feel that they are not being fully developed and supported in their personal and professional growth.

- Reverse mentoring also brings the different employee generations together. The learning that each generation in a company has, is a two-way street.

As with all mentoring programmes, it is important that both parties fully understand and agree to the 'mentoring contract':

- Expectations must be defined. Each party involved in this mentoring partnership must be able to be clear on what they expect from this partnership agreement.

- Willingness from both parties to act as the mentor, as well as the mentee. Both parties must genuinely want to share their information and learn from the other party.

- Respect for the knowledge and experience that each party brings into this relationship. It is very easy to think that the other party doesn't know as much as the first party does; but as a reverse mentoring agreement; both parties must demonstrate the respect for the other party and their knowledge and experience. Both parties have much to gain.

- Trust in moving outside your own comfort zone. This relationship is a two-way street where each party has something to give, as well as something to gain. In gaining more knowledge and experience; the 'learning' party must trust the 'teaching' party to help them understand and trust that they will be pushed outside their comfort zone to try new ways of thinking and working.

- Transparency in that both parties must be open to share their feelings and what they are thinking. If the 'learning' party does not understand, they must say so; and the 'teaching' party must accept what they are being told and find a different way to explain. This is important, as each generation communicates differently; and these differences will come out. The benefit to both parties is that they have the opportunity to see a situation from a different perspective.

Although often this type of mentoring is available within companies, it should not be discounted outside of companies. Two people from different backgrounds can come together and share their knowledge and experience with each other. These backgrounds can be business driven, or cultural, or generation, or language, or hobby/interest specific, or anything that allows two people to come together to learn and benefit from the knowledge and experience of the other. Mentoring of all types should not be restricted, it is important to remember how much each person can learn from someone who is different to themselves.

*"Let your dreams outgrow
the shoes of your expectations."*

Ryunosuke Satoro

The Law of Attraction:
having positive expectations

Research

One of the best-known self-help books of all times is "Think and Grow Rich" by Napoleon Hill, first published in 1937 and selling over 60 million copies. Although this is a very old book, Hill's theory became world news many years later in 2006, when Rhonda Byrne turned it into a movie, and into another book: "The Secret". In short, the theory says that you can expect to have or achieve anything you want, as long as you truly believe that it will happen.

But is that really true?

Many professors have investigated this question, and the outcome is disappointing. Gabrielle Oettingen, Professor of Psychology in New York, researched the power of positive thinking extensively, and she found that those who truly believed in (eg expected) great outcomes consistently performed worse in reality then those who didn't. She beliefs that positive thinking lets our brain believe that we have achieved the outcome already, and therefore sabotages our motivation and willingness to actually achieve the goal. Richard J. Wiseman, Professor of the Public Understanding of Psychology in the UK, goes even further than that, and beliefs that fantasising about the ideal end situation can lead to perfectionism and fear of failure, which stops us from achieving completely. American Social Psychologist Daniel Merton Wegner, who was a Psychology Professor at Harvard, found that conscious positive thinking actually leads to having more negative thoughts.

"Ask someone to think about a red car, and not to think about white bears for the next 5 minutes, and all they will think about is white bears".

Both Wiseman and Wegner belief that this has to with our

evolution as practical human beings. We are programmed to take action to achieve our goals, and to evaluate constantly – and if necessary adjust our plans – along the way to keep moving towards achieving our goal. Wiseman therefore suggest that we should not think about "end goals" but instead about the process, which then inspires action to achieve our goal. If we just believe that we will have a lovely dinner this evening, nothing will happen. If we belief that we will have a lovely dinner this evening, and we think about what we need to do to make that happen (stop at the pizza place), we are more likely to end up with dinner. Wegner explains that if we are instructed not to think about white bears, we will check constantly if we aren't thinking about white bears, and the effect is: we think about the white bears constantly!

So, if that's the case, then why should you even bother with trying to stay positive, making positive affirmations, and setting up your mind to expect that good will happen? Well, because other research shows that all these actions can actually benefit us as well!

Barbara Fredrickson, a positive psychology researcher at the University of Carolina, proved through research that positive thinking opens up our brains. When we feel angry, anxious or sad, our minds will narrow and start focusing on these threats to help overcome them. But when we think positive thoughts and feel happy and content, our minds will open up, and we will see more opportunity and possibility. We may all recognise this from spending time on vacation, where all of a sudden great new ideas or solutions to long standing problems may come to us.

And have you ever experienced that your senses focus on

whatever is on your mind as well? When you have a crush, all of a sudden you will see signs of that crush anywhere. You may discover that the whole world seems to drive the same car, wear the same jacket, has the same walk, etc. When you are renovating your house, all of a sudden you notice all the great things that other people have done with their houses, which you never noticed before because you simply weren't zoomed in on it. And the same goes for achieving your personal goals: when you think about the goals, your senses will open up to spot ideas, opportunities, and solutions related to that goal.

As an added bonus, but not the least important, a study published by Harvard in 2017 showed that positive thinking improves our health and significantly lowers the risk of some diseases, and cardiovascular disease in particular. The researchers even go as far as to state that high optimism results in a lower risk of death!

So, whatever the proven pro's and con's may be, we would encourage you to think positive and – within reason - always expect the best, as this will not only help you forward in life, but it may also contribute to living a longer and happier life!

http://www.psychologisch.nu/marcelino/hoe-positief-denken-negatief-uitpakt

https://jamesclear.com/positive-thinking

https://news.harvard.edu/gazette/story/2016/12/optistic-women-live-longer-are-healthier/

Expectations

Take Action!

Expectation is simply defined as believing that something you want or don't want is going to happen. It is also believing that something should happen or not happen in a certain way.

Expectations are all about what you focus on. If you focus on what you don't want to happen, it will happen. If you focus on what you do want to happen, it will happen. You try and fit your life into your expectations, and this is the reason expectations can hurt you. If you turn this around and create your expectations; by taking action today, you can make your expectations motivate you.

Take Action!

1. Create your list of expectations. Take a clean page in your journal and start to write out your expectations, leaving space to answer the questions below. It is important when you are thinking about your expectations that you take into account every situation and every person involved in your life.

2. Take each part of your life one at a time. For example:

   • Start with your family and then move onto your friends. Taking your immediate family (significant other and children); what do you expect from them?

   • Then expand out to the next level – what do you expect from your parents? Then what do you expect from your cousins and their families?

   • Then ask yourself 'what do I expect from my friends?'

- Move onto your work or business life. What do you expect from your career? What do you expect from your boss? What do you expect from your colleagues? What do you expect from your staff? What do you expect from your clients?

- Move onto the services you have, for example from your doctor, dentist, resident's council, government departments, library, children's teachers / lecturers, telephone company, internet provider, mobile / cell phone provider, insurance company, and the list goes on.

3. Take some of the more problematic relationships you have. What do you expect from these relationships?

4. Take some of the happier relationships you have. What do you expect from these relationships?

5. What do you expect from your life?

It does not matter how long your list is, keep writing down your expectations until you think that you have written them all down. Against each expectation, ask yourself the following questions:

1. Does this expectation make me happy?

2. What made me have this expectation in the first place?

3. Does what really happens to me, meet my expectation?

4. If what happens does not meet my expectations, why do I have this expectation?

5. Do I expect too much, or do I expect too little?

6. Who is responsible for my expectation?

7. How can I make this expectation work for me?

It is very important that we meet our own expectations, after all this is where you spend your time and your energy. If you are spending time and energy on relationships that are not meeting your expectations, you are spending time and energy on something that isn't working for you or supporting you.

When you work through all these questions, and the underlying reason for your expectation becomes clearer, you can then ask yourself the last question: How can I make this expectation work for me? It may be that this is working for you, but maybe the person you have this expectation of isn't the right person. It may be that this expectation is not working for you and you need to change your expectation.

Only you have full responsibility over your own expectations. It is easy to blame someone else when something doesn't go the way you expect it to; but who set that level of expectation?

Here's the challenge though; what about the expectations you have of others? Are they aware of your expectations of them? An easy example of this is when you first meet your significant other and they bring you flowers every Saturday. You have set the expectation in you that they will always bring you flowers every Saturday. What happens when they don't?

As you work your way through creating this list and then

analysing it with the questions, you may find that some of this is painful. That is not the intention. The intention is to help you become aware of, and take responsibility for, your own expectations.

Remember, these are your expectations and you can change them.

*"Action is the foundational key
to all success."*

Pablo Picasso

Annual Performance Review Feedback:

"*managing expectations*"

QUESTION EVERYTHING

Your Questions Answered

Dear Amarantine Team,

Last week, I had one of my most dreaded days of the year at work; it was time again for my annual performance review.

I always get very nervous around this time of the year. All of a sudden, I start remembering all the mistakes that I've made over the year, and I feel insecure. Yet at the same time, I also start focussing on the pay increase negotiations, desperately searching for reasons to justify my request, which I then can't find. And I even get sort of angry in advance about how this conversation may turn downhill real fast. But the worst of it is; it never turns out like that. I usually have a very pleasant and constructive conversation, with lots of positive feedback on my performance, and a nice pay increase as a result!

This year was no different, it was all positive. I really only got one remark in terms of improving my performance, and that was that I should get better at "managing expectations". Now, I know what my manager means by this, and it was no surprise, as I've heard it before. But my problem is, I have no clue where to start on improving this. I just don't see how I can be responsible for other people's thoughts.

So, my question to your team is, do you have any ideas on how I can take this feedback forward and actually do so something with it?

Many thanks,
Iris McCain, Dublin, Ireland

Dear Iris,

Although people's private thought processes, and therefore their individual expectations, are everyone's own responsibility, managing expectations is a rather important skill on the work floor (and can be very helpful in your private life as well!).

Basically, we all manage other people's expectations on a daily basis. Sometimes we do that in a very obvious way; by making promises. When you promise someone to do something, they will expect you to deliver on that promise. And when you don't follow through, people will feel disappointed, or might even get angry, because their expectations are unmet.

It becomes a bit trickier when we don't make an explicit promise, and people still have expectations. This is usually a result of common practice, habits, etc. As an example, if you always arrive at the office early, people will get to expect that you'll be there, and will be surprised, worried, disappointed or get angry when all of a sudden you turn up late. You may not have made any promises to be there early, but people have become to rely on you to be there anyway because that's how things have been going for some time.

So, the key to managing other people's expectations really is communication. You need to be mindful of what's going on in terms of common practice and habits, you need to clarify what other people are expecting from you by asking them questions, and you need to be clear on what you can (or can't) deliver and live up to that once you've made a promise.

So, back to your original question, you will need to check

what others at work expect from you and why they expect that, and then you can start figuring out what you'll have to do or communicate to either meet or change those expectations.

Warmest regards,
The Amarantine Team

Introduction

It's all in the Numbers!

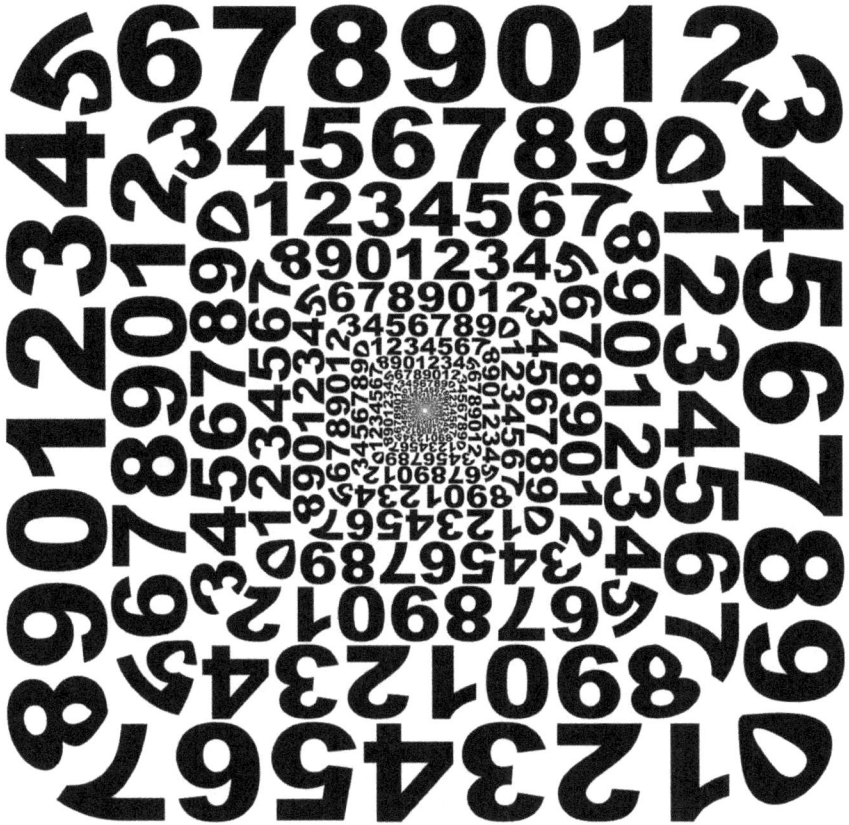

Numerology Series
by
Loren Schmal

For anyone who is interested, curious or even a true believer, the basic definition of numerology is the universal language of numbers. By breaking down the patterns of the universe into numbers, we are able to uncover information about the world as a whole, as well as every individual. Numerology is the science of numbers, but it only involves simple mathematics.

It's more about the personalities of each number, and how each numbers' traits alter the course of your life depending on where they appear in your personal Numerology - if they appear at all. Numerology is a tool used to investigate our own very being, and to bring light our highest potential on the physical, emotional, mental and spiritual planes. Numerology tells of our potential destiny, our natural talents and helps us gain a better understanding of ourselves and others. It shows us the pathway we need to take in our lives to fulfill this potential, and also, tells us one of the many reasons why each one has different traits and characteristics. Numbers have been in existence since the beginning of time and predates all Alphabets.

Each number has a different vibration, and can therefore give us a better understanding of one's pathway, and the circumstances which surround our life. It can direct one to the career best suited to each person, and gives us the opportunity to be more aware of the talents we have and of the pathways we choose to utilize them. It also tells us of the compatibility we have with another, especially who would be most compatible as a partner for you. It tells you how you may best help your family and friends, due to the numbers which control their lives.

Each number is influenced by a different planet in our Solar

System. Each letter of the alphabet vibrates to a given number, 1 – 9, which is also the span of our life cycles. The numbers under which we were born, plus the numbers in our names, are the tools that we are given in order that we may accomplish our mission in life, and enable us to work through all our Karmic Lessons. The Vibratory Power of each number affects us in both Positive and Negative ways.

HOW TO WORK OUT
YOUR OWN NUMEROLOGY

The symbolic meanings that surround the nine whole numbers are the centre of Numerological divination. Numbers are also keyed to letters of the alphabet, so words and names, as well as dates of birth, can be analysed.

Numerology in
Relation to the Alphabet

Each letter of the alphabet is represented by a number between 1 and 9.

1	–	A	J	S
2	–	B	K	T
3	–	C	L	U
4	–	D	M	V
5	–	E	N	W
6	–	F	O	X
7	–	G	P	Y
8	–	H	Q	Z
9	–	I	R	

NAME NUMEROLOGY

The First Name is our 'Foundation in Life'.

To find the total Numerological vibration of your name, translate the letters of your name into the numbers as listed above, and add those number together. Then, break down the result in separate numbers, which you add up again, until you have reduced it to a single digit number. This number is known as your Name Ruling Number.

As an example, let's take the name Chantel. This name translates to C=3, H=8, A=1, N=5, T=2, E=5, L=3.

When we add those numbers (3+8+1+5+2+5+3) we get to 27.

As this is a double digit, which we still need to reduce to 1 digit, we add the numbers of this result.

So: 2+7=9.

The Name Ruling Number for the name Chantel is therefore 9.

DATE OF BIRTH NUMEROLOGY

DAY NUMBER

Your Day Number is the energy which influences who you are and all that you do in your life, on a daily basis. It tells of what makes you respond and act as you do, and is an indication of what type of life you should lead in order to be successful in all that you undertake in this lifetime.

Your Day Number is the day of your birth.

Using as an example the 26th of September 1967, the Day Number is 26 = 2 + 6 = 8.

8 is the Day Number.

DESTINY NUMBER

The destiny number is one of the most important numbers on your chart. It is the ruling force that describes what you must do/learn, in order to operate harmoniously with your environment and how you can get the most out of your present life. It shows the direction you must take, representing the only opportunities for success that will be made available to you.

To analyse and interpret your 'Destiny Number', simply use the formula of reducing your entire date of birth to a single digit.

For example, the 'Destiny Number' for a person with the date of birth of the 26th of September 1967 is
2+6+0+9+1+9+6+7 = 40,
4+0 = 4.

PERSONAL YEAR

The Personal Year Number is the energy by which you will live your life from your birthday of this year, until your birthday of next year. This is the vibration that will influence all that you do throughout that period.

The Personal Year energy is present from birthday to birthday. To work out your Personal Year Number, take the Day and Month Numbers and add them to the Year Number.

For example, the Personal Year Number in 2018 for someone with the date of birth 26/09/1967 would be Number 1. Add the day and month numbers to the year number (2018)
2+6+0+9+2+0+1+8 = 28:
2 + 8 = 10:
1+0=1, making 1 the Personal Year Number.

Loren Schmal
© 2018 Loren Schmal

Founder of CyberPA

It's all in the Numbers!

Numerology Series
by
Loren Schmal

Number 1

The numerology meaning of the number 1 – The Primal Force.

In Numerology, each of the nine single-digit numbers has a personality; a limited range of qualities and traits that makes it unique and recognizable. To me, each number is a character, like any human being. In order to understand how numbers affect us, based on their location in the chart, it helps to get to know each single digit number as if it were a person.

The goal is to get beyond each number being just a list of positive and negative qualities and to, instead, make each number come alive and to sense how the numbers play off of each other. If you sense some exaggeration in my descriptions, remember that these nine "individuals" are extremes by their very nature (while we, as human beings, are made up of a mixture of all the numbers' traits).

Among the nine single-digit numbers, the 1 takes a special place. From a spiritual perspective, it is the number of creation, the primal force from which all other numbers spring forth (as opposed to the often quoted zero from which, by definition, nothing could possibly come into being).

It is said that when you truly understand the place and function of this most primal of all numbers, you will know all there is to know and enlightenment is yours. This statement, of course, does not apply to an understanding of the number 1 from a Numerologist's perspective alone, but perhaps that is a good place to start, as the personality of the number 1 aligns nicely with its more elevated spiritual symbolism.

The 1 is a doer, a powerful force that produces results and does not allow anything or anyone to limit its potential. The 1 is aggressive, a necessary energy for creating and producing. The 1 is always in the forefront: a spearpoint directing and leading others. The shape of the number 1, just like the shape of all other symbols, reflects its meaning; it walks upright with pride and purpose. Strong, determined, unwavering and with specific goals in mind, the 1 can turn dreams and ideas into reality. It pushes obstacles aside or simply drills right through them.

The 1 grows, transforms and improves in perpetuity, precisely the way Mother Nature does. After all, nature's primal force and most basic building block is the number 1. Nature knows no mercy and its cruelty can be heartbreaking. However, it knows balance and gives life indiscriminately and without judgment. Scientists sometimes compete with nature, genetically altering fruits or breeding bugs for specific purposes. An understanding of nature teaches us that this is never a good idea and almost always produces unexpected backlashes. The number 1 has a similar built-in perfection and balance; you can force a change here or there, but negative repercussions are likely.

The 1 tends to have a simple, straightforward view of life and its many complexities. It trusts its own ability to separate right from wrong. It doesn't waste time on abstract ideas or anything else that isn't in line with its pursuit of results. The 1 is no preacher, no philosopher, no spiritual explorer, no dreamer and certainly not an idealist. It is a pragmatist, a ruthless conqueror and a warrior extraordinaire. It is individualistic and independent to a

1

What is Number 1:
- in your Life Challenges?
- as a Personal Year?
- as Destiny Number?

How does number 1
help, support, impact your CAREER?

What COLOUR
is associated with number 1?

What does it mean if you find a Number 1
in your own numbers?

fault. It will attempt to force its values and opinions on you but it won't accept, or even listen to, yours.

The 1 does not hesitate when it senses a need for confrontation. It is jealous and extremely stubborn, but also courageous and willing to try anything new if it sees promise, even at great danger. It is, if you haven't guessed, the most masculine of all numbers. There is a certain quality, a sense of honour and responsibility that demands our respect, and it has a sense of justice that cannot be denied. The number 1 cannot witness injustice without jumping in and setting things straight.

Its purity of purpose is an admirable quality of the number 1. It sees things for what they are and hypocrisy doesn't stand a chance. Befriend a 1 and you have a friend for life. You can poke fun at a 1 and not have to worry about hurt feelings. A 1 has a great capacity for humour, including the self-deprecating kind. If, however, you try to cater to a 1 to win its love or friendship, you'll lose its respect instead. Stand up to a 1 and you may lose the fight, but you'll gain its admiration. If you are in trouble and need help, the number 1 is who you want on your side -- there is no more dedicated protector or braver partner. If you are in love, the number 1 is the most difficult of all lovers: demanding, jealous, confrontational and impatient. If you find yourself in the service of a 1, you will be pushed to the limit, abused at all hours, and incapable of living up to its expectations.

But you will also, without a doubt, become the best you could ever be. If the 1 is your enemy, you will be crushed without mercy.

If you yourself are a 1, your happiness and satisfaction will come from your work more than from any other source. And if it was possible for a person to be fully and truly a 1 and only a 1, that individual would be successful and intimidating, as well as extremely unpleasant and dangerous.

What does it mean if you find a Number 1 in your own numbers?

In our Introduction to Numerology we've explained how you can calculate your own numbers. Have any of your numbers turned out to be a 1? If yes, then please find below an explanation as to what this means.

COLOURS associated with number 1

Number 1's should include the colour yellow in their lives as it is a bold colour that represents success.

Red is also a colour that vibrates with the number 1 as it is the colour of action and passion.

Number 1 LIFE CHALLENGES

People with a life challenge Number 1 may feel as if every dream and ambition that they have is being thwarted by unfair circumstances. Bitterness, defensiveness and blaming others may be a chronic problem. Usually this is due to being too pushy or aggressive. Even if you are not unreliable or unpredictable, others may perceive you as so. A gentler touch plus a well-focused, methodical plan can help you achieve your aims. You self-sabotage by plunging ahead blindly.

1 as a DAY NUMBER

You are independent, a born leader, ambitious and a high achiever. A highly original thinker with great ideas, you have the initiative to begin new things.

Number 1 as Destiny Number

Positive Characteristics:

People born with the 1 Destiny Number are decisive and independent. They make strong and effective leaders as they are assertive, confident and perceptive.

Number 1's often reach the top in their chosen careers because they are self-motivated and focused on success. They are often of higher than average intelligence and use this to their advantage. Destiny number 1's is strongly linked with creativity and originality.

A number 1 is usually blessed with motivation, enthusiasm, creativity and inspiration. They tend to be physically healthier and mentally stronger than most other people are.

Your purpose is to set good examples of success through determination, and show others how to be strong.

Negative Characteristics:

People born with the Destiny Number 1 can tend to be self-centred and have narrow vision as a result of their self-confidence and determination to succeed.

They can be rather tyrannical in their attempts to lead, and other people often regard them as domineering and dictatorial. Number 1's are not good at negotiating and can be stubborn and co-operative. This means that, despite their confidence and ambition, they do not possess good leadership skills. Number 1's can be their own worst enemies if they set themselves unachievable goals that cannot be met. This in turn can lead to frustration. 1 often lusts for success (especially material) at any cost.

Your challenge is to curb your selfishness and ego.

Number 1 as a PERSONAL YEAR

Planting Seeds, Rebirth, Beginning of An Era

This is a new beginning time. Embrace courage, openness, and initiate new ideas. Energy is behind you supporting new directions and self-definition, so follow your dreams and begin cultivating what really motivates you. Begin manifesting and attracting what you want into your life.

Number 1 signifies taking on new challenges so don't be afraid to extend yourself in the direction you wish to go in. You'll be fully supported by the energies of the Universe. It is not a time to wait around as you could miss out on what this year has to offer. You really are setting the pace for the next nine years, so make sure the direction you choose is the direction you really want for the future.

This is the beginning of a new nine-year cycle and things that have concerned you for the past decade no longer matter at all, in fact you may find your priorities have changed altogether.

Disappointments from the past simply don't matter

anymore. You have bigger fish to fry, and any work that you do during this year sets the tone and foundation for the next nine. This is the time to decide what your goals are and act on them. It is time to take control of your life. You must take responsibility for yourself, and trust that you have the insight to call the right shots. Take advice, but think it over yourself before following anything. If it seems wrong, trust your instincts and follow your own heart. You'll know what's right for you.

A 1 Personal Year is a powerful year for adjustments, as would be expected after the dynamic year 9. It is a year of new beginnings and adjustments on all levels, and it is a time to gain inner strength. It is also a time to take the lead and assert one's self.

You can, throughout this year, have many feelings of isolation and aloneness; so it would be wise at these times to raise the awareness with meditation and the like at any opportunity. This will also allow you to find peace and security within. It is also a time to enjoy one's own space to look at enjoying and living your freedom and allowing others to do the same. A 1 Personal Year also often brings new vitality and physical strength.

A Personal Year of 1 which represents taking complete control of your life and heading in the direction of your choosing.

Number 1 in CAREER

A leader, risk-taker and original thinker, you have great drive and can succeed against all the odds. Destiny Number 1's are suited to careers that make the most of their creative talents, but also allow them the opportunity to excel and succeed. You are able to excel anywhere you can display your leadership qualities. Number 1's often become great leaders and for this reason, and they make great entrepreneurs, freelancers, generals, commanders, CEOs and producers. Writer, director, inventor, president, public figure, business owner, designer, architect, composer, professor, teacher, veterinarian, minister, psychologist, artist, dentist, healing, politician, sportsperson, team leader, fashion designer, teacher, doctor, chiropractor, minister, lawyer, FBI, curator of a museum.

Loren Schmal
© 2018 Loren Schmal

Founder of CyberPA

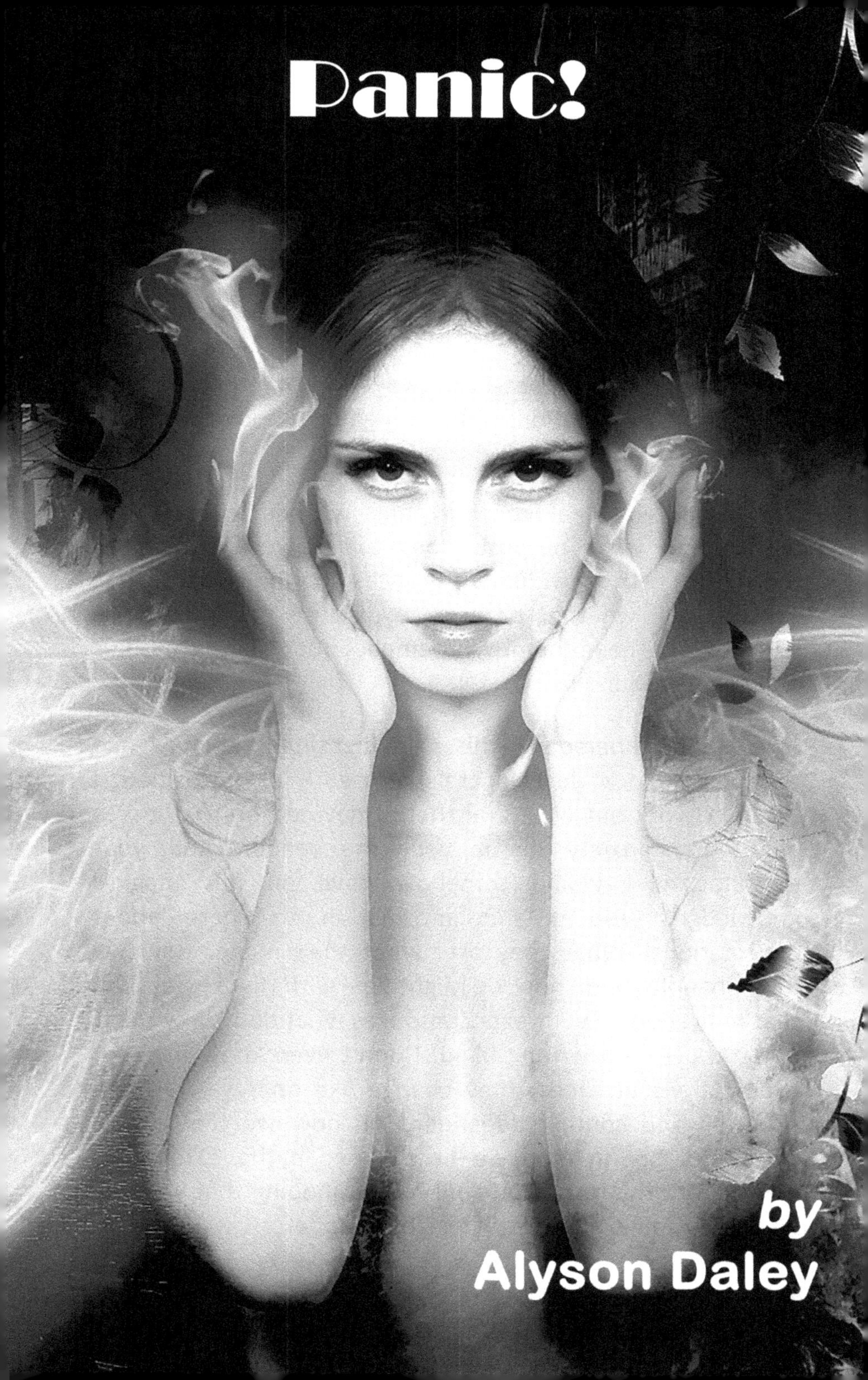
Panic!
by
Alyson Daley

Expectation in Psychology is a belief about what will happen in the future.

We all have expectations, then we panic depending on if they are high or low. Can we can meet our expectations or not? To what degree can we meet our expectations, is the glass half full or empty?

What about the expectations we have of other people? What if the expectations are too high or too low, what will that mean to and/or for us?

We have this internal feeling of panic, worry or anxiety. Why is this and what purpose does this serve? We are all individuals with individual differences and individual needs. Yet we still, whether or not we disclose or share those expectations, have them. What impact does that have on us and others around us?

I know, for me personally this is the first time that I have had a writer's block. Just for this article. I just struggled. I couldn't work out why, and then it dawned on me. It was about my anxiety about you, the reader, and your expectation. I would somehow have all this magical knowledge, wisdom and information to share about expectations! What they are, what they mean, how we might handle them, how we might deal with them – yet I felt that I fell short of your expectation, as what do I know that I don't know I am writing blind. I don't even know my own expectations at times; they change like energy. They are situation and context dependent on how we feel at any given moment in time. So here I am, in the 11th hour, pouring out my heart and soul to you, hoping that you will be able to gain a glimmer of insight or hope.

I knew I would eventually get there, but my own expectations kept me frozen, on lock down. Why, you may ask? You may relate to this immobilised state in your own way. For me, I feel the biggest part is the constraints, the cage they place upon me, and on you. Now I don't mean expectations of working your 8-hour shift, stopping at a red light; as these are more about breaking the law, injuring someone or yourself or even death; the other is if you don't go into work, you do not get paid.

For me personally and professionally there are set expectations in delivering a Higher Education Degree. These expectations are to teach the students to a point where they are understanding the information, able to write assignments, sit exams and passing them (and hopefully to a good standard!). However, for me, I want my students to enjoy the topic, the subject, internalise it, grow, develop. Now this is not an expectation; this is a hope, a passion, a desire for all my students; this is about their personal and professional academic journey. I am sure this may sound fluffy and romantic, yet you imagine how far a person could grow and develop given an environment with hope coupled with healthy expectations.

Expectations – a confident belief or strong hope that a particular event will happen.

In case of uncertainty, we - as naive scientists (Heider, 1958) - try and make sense of our world and to reduce the uncertainty. We need certain information about what we are to expect, what is expected of and from us, because they importantly affect the way we behave towards each other. This is called interpersonal relations; for most parts we react to what another person is perceiving and feeling, and also may be doing. In other words, as Heider states, this is 'the presumed events inside another person's (skin) head', which usually enters as features of the relation; in other words, meaningful connection or association. Therefore, expectations frequently guide our behaviour and make it easier to predict what will happen next.

For example, if you have attended a charity ball previously, you know the pre-set expectations such as dress code, donations, and expected behaviour. We have a set of expectations based on prior knowledge when we are going to the dentist, the doctors, or somewhere similar. Going to see our best friend, our beloved relatives; these are however, less formal situations with expectations nonetheless, these are called construction constructs (corollary).

In my job there is, as with all other jobs, expectations. I have come across the saying 'teachers have a right to teach, students have a right to learn' (Darling-Hammond, 1997); straight away expectations are set. Tuition fees are so high. Students are human capital, a commodity. More and more is expected from the lecturers by the student. Think about this, 'if you help someone and expect something in return' you are doing business. Think about my point above. They are buying from us, the institution; so the expectations are high. Market place skills, institutional expectations.

Blame the Conditions of Worth

What does all of this mean and why do we have expectations? Whose expectation are they? Yours! Mine! My expectation of what I think you are expecting or vice versa?

Just to reiterate, we are all individuals, have individual differences and individual needs. Yet, whether or not we choose to disclose or share those expectations, we all have them.

What are your expectations reading this magazine? That one, some, or all authors will impart some knowledge or information, answers that will resonate with you, ignite a fire within? How would you feel if those expectations were not met? Who would you blame? The authors? The magazine? What would be the rationale for that blame? That it didn't ignite, meet or live up to your expectations? However, that is you placing your conditions of worth on to me and on to the team. That is you not taking responsibility for your own expectations, the actions that follow and your internal belief system.

So we all have expectations and those expectations can be wrapped up in conditions of worth. Conditions of worth are what have been placed upon us during our lifespan of early development. We then go on to create our own conditions of worth through our own independent living. However, whether we realise it or not, want to admit it or not, we still have within us those conditions of worth from our past life. They could be seen as our core conditions of worth, ones that were placed upon us without choice, and we kick against them.

I feel, for me this has been part of my block to writing this article. I hate (hate is a strong word and believe me, I do not use it lightly) the negative conditions of worth that were placed upon me, and I have worked so long and hard to change and develop these to positive ones. Then all of a sudden they rear their ugly head. Expectations; demands; which were placed upon me, and then me and my expectations of others. This caused me angst, and frustration. I feel, because they were placed on me, I had to meet these expectations. I also demanded them of others and WO-betide anyone that didn't meet them. It became about respect, principles, being a good person, so if you didn't meet my expectations then it meant in my eyes that you didn't respect me. In fact, it demonstrated a huge disrespect. In other words; you were telling me 'I was not worthy'.

Personally and professionally, I have challenged expectations and what constraints they place on us all. I have learnt and unlearned about many things; one being expectations. Is it truly healthy to place such a heavy burden on someone? "We expect you to pass your exams son." "I expect you to say you love me when I tell you." "I expect that you will listen when I talk." "I expect that you will agree with me, because I am your parent, your boss, your partner."

You don't have to stop at a red light, but be prepared for the consequences. Now that is not me placing an expectation, this is about consequences of our actions.

What you want, what you give, is it what I need; or is it what you think I need.

Alyson Daley
© 2018 Alyson Daley

Lecturer in Psychology (University of Huddersfield and Bradford College), Huddersfield Change Project volunteer, Mental Health Practitioner, and Energy Mover

*"The main thing in making art
often is letting go of
your expectation and your idea."*

Agnes Martin

I am not in this world to live up to your expectations, and you are not in this world to live up to mine

......

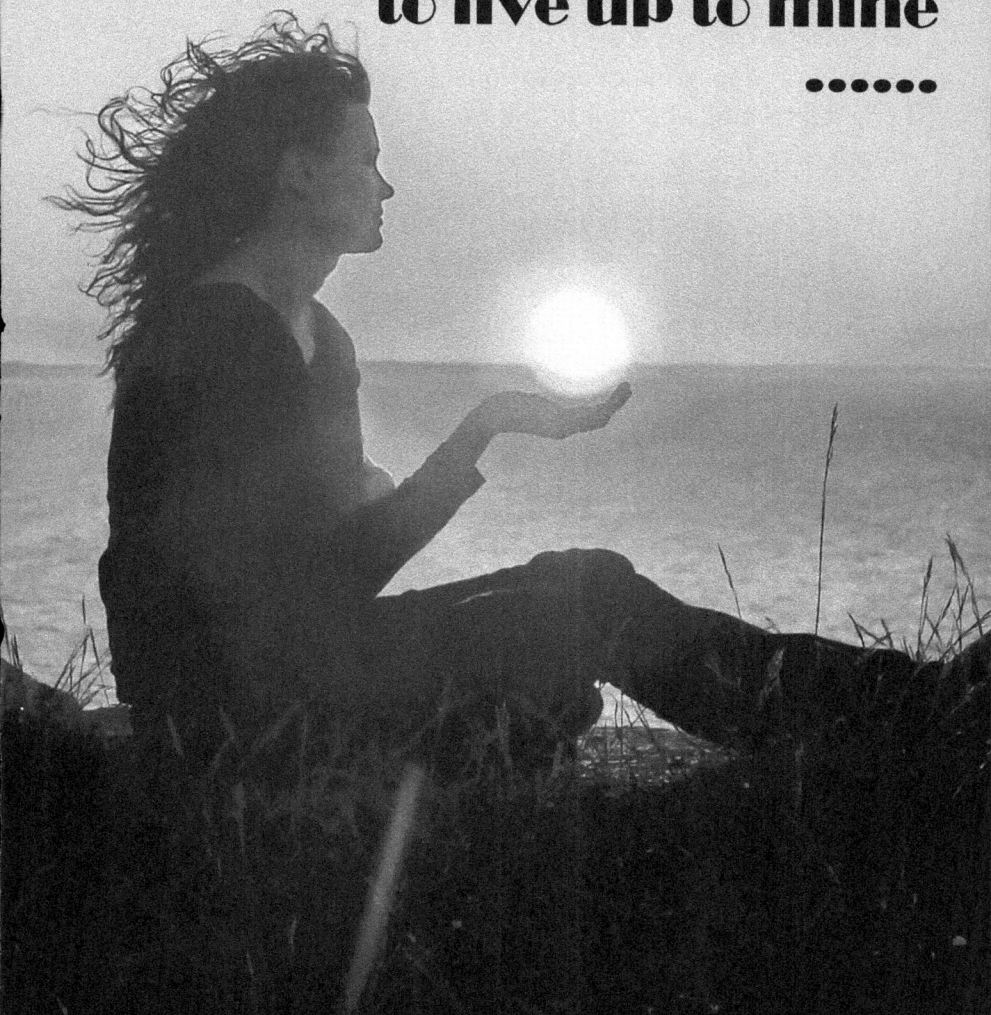

by
Charuni Senanayake

I had too many thoughts related to 'expectations' and struggled to get my ideas sorted out to write this article. I was wondering why? How come I can be so tangled in my own emotions that I couldn't quite pin point what to share!

As I looked back I understood; it was because I had a tug-of-war inside me, on views of having high expectations and lowering the existing expectations. I decided to start simple. I started to look at some of the famous Quotes. Surely, it did wonders to figuring out my own thoughts....

"The secret to happiness is low expectations".
Barry Schewartz

"There are ways to be happy - improve your reality or lower your expectations".
PictureQuotes.com

"Expectations are pre mediated resentments".
Anonymous

"Sometimes you just have to lower your expectations to avoid unnecessary disappointments".
Anonymous

"Expectation is the root of all heartache".
Shakespeare

"Keep your expectations
high on achievement and low on people".
Anonymous

"Let your dreams
outgrow the shoes of your expectations".
Ryunosuke Satoro

"I am not in this world to live up to your expectations

and you are not in this world to live up to mine".
Bruce Lee

While there were many quotes on lowering expectations, there were very few written on having expectations. Throughout all, my favorite was Bruce Lee's Quote. I saw such value behind those words. Clarity of my own jumbled feelings slowly started to move into place, a piece of the mind puzzle moved to where it belonged.

I would like to ask you a question. **Do you feel like you are 'living'?**

When I asked myself this question, truthfully I understood the answer to it was 'I don't feel like I am living'. Sometime ago I have put my life into the 'default' mode, rather than customizing it the way that I wanted. Lots of things have come on my way and I haven't chosen the most important aspects of my life, I haven't realized the areas I wanted to say 'No' to, I have just passed time in the recent past feeling overwhelmed. I could see in my mind's eye, even though I blamed others for my circumstances, deep within I knew it's me who needs to take responsibility for it. I stopped living for a while.

This realization of my present life shed light in terms of expectations. I realized that most of the time I have lowered my expectations on many aspects of my life, to avoid feelings of disappointment, hurt, lack of control, etc. I have probably lowered my expectations more often than I had expectations for myself. I had forgotten that I should have primarily lowered expectations of others, but perhaps i shouldn't have my lowered expectations of my own self. However, it has happened in both ways, and without realizing this I had settled my life mode to 'default'.

Getting my thoughts in order and reflecting on each situation, I started to look at ways how I could feel like 'living' again. I learnt the following during this change process:

1. Design your life whenever and where ever you can: Identify if you have set the mode of life to 'default', following a deep analysis of and reflection on things around you. How you are feeling, what you have, what you would like to have etc. Stop hiding behind other people's decisions, traditions, and cultures. Don't let others tell you what you should be doing with your life. Take responsibility for designing your own journey every step of the way. Feel your passions and take actions to achieve them. You may actually get a chance to create your life, by doing things that touch or move you, rather than sitting in one place and wishing for something to happen. Even if you do not succeed fully, you will know that you had the guts to try, and that you've gained lots of positive experiences that enrich your life in different aspects.

2. When you try to do 'hard' things, great opportunities also will come your way: Willingness to accept and grow during hard periods of life shows your character, your dedication and how strong you are as a person. Remember the saying 'Best things in life are hard to come by'? If you lower your expectations of yourself and shy away from the difficulty of the situation, you may miss out on them entirely. Learning a new area of work, skill building, building a business, having a successful marriage or bringing up successful kids can all be hard. But if you become good in doing hard things, you may become good in doing almost everything, and your

success rate at anything you try will be much higher.

3. Expect that small things lay the foundation to bigger things in life:
    One of the articles I recently read had the following sentence which I believe says it all: 'You can't lift a thousand pounds all at once, but you can lift one pound a thousand times'. I know why I have been unhappy and impatient many times in my life, I expected results just that minute, and wanted them instantly. This leads to frustration and all sorts of negative feelings. Small, dedicated, repeated efforts will get you their eventually.

4. Don't expect you will win life, just by moving forward only:
    There are times when we go around and come back to a dead end. Maybe in that case it may be worth identifying that we may not be on the right path. Maybe it is time to move backwards, re-assess and take a U turn. There is absolutely a big difference when you decide to give up on one thing, and start over in the right direction.

5. The biggest disappointments in life come when you had put unrealistic expectations in place:
    It's our perception of things, or it's our judgment according to our experiences, that makes us set the standards and expectations for how something 'should be'. The minute we change our perception of things and how we look at them, we see things in a different light, without unnecessary stress and frustration. Have a positive attitude and open mind, and you will be able to clearly see the difference between an unrealistic expectation and an expectation that helps you move forward.

Last but not least, it's about managing our expectations. Choosing the areas where to have higher expectations and choosing the areas where to have lower expectations, looking at things openly and mindfully and being non-judgmental, where it can help us to live again and be happy. Today, I truly believe in that we were NOT brought to this world to live up to other peoples' expectations, but to craft our own journey and achieve to the highest purpose for what we were chosen for.

Charuni Senanayake

© 2018 Dr Charuni Senanayake

Life Coach,
Executive Coach
and
Coach Trainer

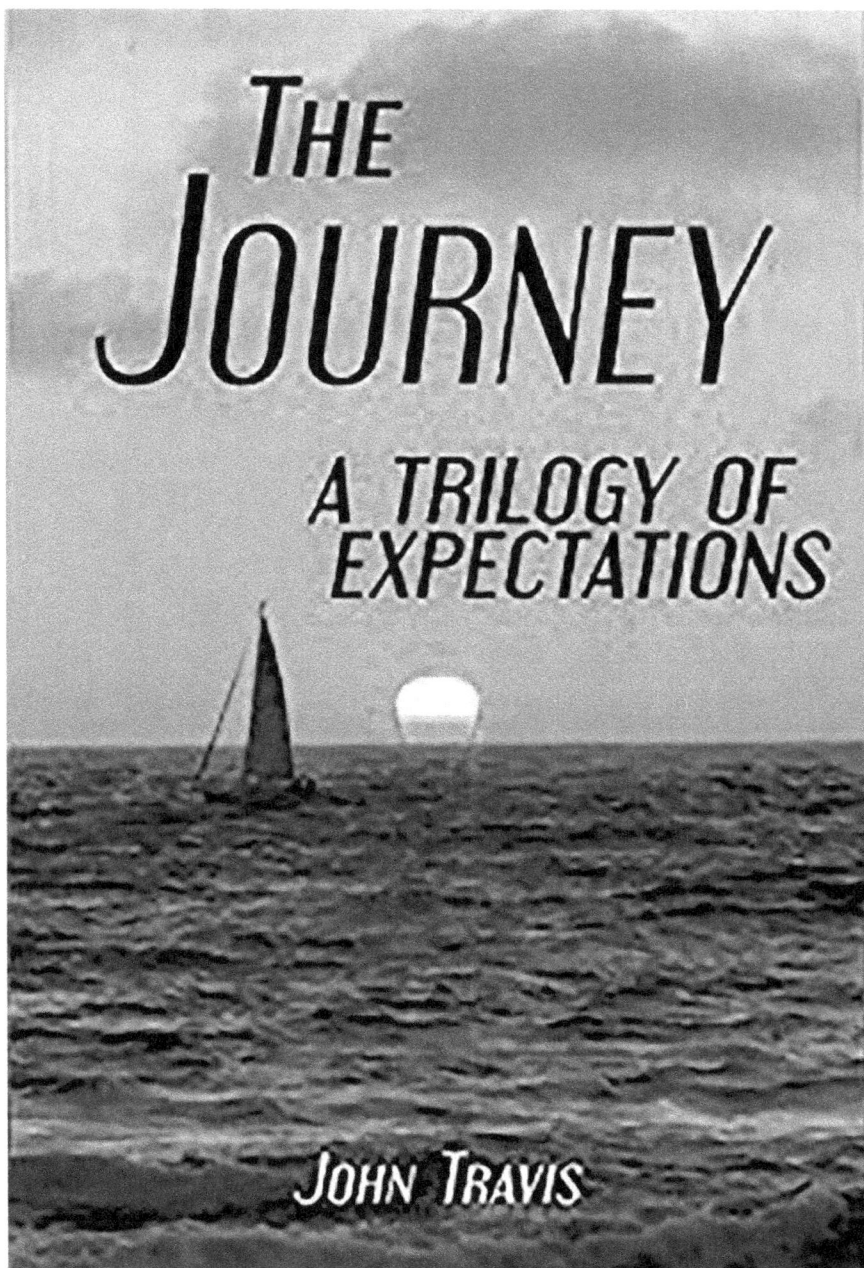

Welcome to your Personal & Professional Development with Amarantine

Amarantine supports your Personal and Professional Development through assessing, exploring, developing, and inspiring yourself to increase your self-awareness, self-knowledge, self-confidence, and self-esteem; to help you identify and develop your talents, skills, knowledge, competence, and experience to fulfil your personal aspirations in both your personal and professional life, to provide you with an enhanced lifestyle and improved quality of life as a result.

Whether you have a personal goal or a professional career goal, Amarantine will answer the questions you ask in an inspirational manner that helps you take the next step to achieve your own personal and professional aspirations.

Amarantine supports lifelong learning; which is achieved through both formal and informal learning processes. Formal learning is defined as education and training; whereas informal learning comes from coaching, mentoring, supervision, as well as things you experience, see, and hear in your everyday life.

Amarantine will inspire you to consciously learn and develop in all areas of your personal and professional life.

www.Amarantine.Life